Friends of the Wolf

Robert Young

Real Writing Press

Friends with a Wolf?

Meet Canis lupis, a gray wolf. It looks like a dog, but it isn't. It's a wild animal.

To survive, wolves must hunt and kill. Working together, they search their territory for prey. The pack chases down the prey, surrounds it, and attacks. Using their razor-sharp teeth, the wolves rip open the animal and eat it.

Canis lupus is the scientific name for the gray wolf. Scientists organize all living things using Latin names.

Wolves have 42 teeth (we have 32), each with a special job. Canine teeth, which can be up to 2.5 inches (6 cm) long, are used to grab and to tear. Molars are used for grinding. The wolf's bite force is so strong it can crush the thighbone of a moose.

Wolves' favorite food? Ungulates—animals with hooves—like deer, elk, bison, and moose. But wolves aren't picky. They will also eat rabbits, raccoons, beavers, voles, mice, and even fish! If they can't find wild animals to eat, wolves may attack cows, sheep, goats, dogs, and cats. Look out! Wolves could even attack people.

Wolves are wild and dangerous animals. **Who would dare be *friends* with them?**

Think you can outrun a wolf? They run fast—nearly 40 miles (64 km) an hour—for short distances (the fastest human has run 27.8 miles/44.7 km) an hour. Wolves trot at 5 miles (8 km) an hour and can travel up to 50 miles (80 km) a day.

The Amazing Wolf

Plenty of people would dare to be friends with wolves, and for good reasons. Wolves are smart and strong. They are skilled hunters with spectacular senses! Wolves can detect movement a mile (1.6 km) away. They can hear sounds from five to ten miles (8-16 km). And their sense of smell? A hundred times better than ours!

Wolves are social animals, like us. They live in groups, called packs, and they work together and play together. Wolves don't talk, but they can communicate well using sounds and their body language.

Packs range in size from as few as two to as many as 36 wolves. The average size is six to eight.

Wolves' voices help them communicate. Barking and growling are warnings. Wolves whine when they want something and whimper when they are giving in to another wolf. Each wolf has a unique howl. They howl to keep other wolves away or to find each other. They do not howl at the moon!

Every pack has a ranking system. There are leaders, dominant wolves, and followers, subordinate wolves. All use body language to show their rank. Which of these wolves is the dominant one? How can you tell?

Dominant wolves stand erect. They point their ears upward and hold their tails high. Around dominant wolves, subordinates will crouch. They hold their ears back and tuck their tails.

This is another posture subordinate wolves use.

But, aren't wolves dangerous to humans? Don't they attack people? Yes, wolves have attacked people, but those attacks are very, very rare. Mostly, wolves are afraid of people so they hide or run away.

You are much more likely to be hit by lightning than bitten by a wolf.

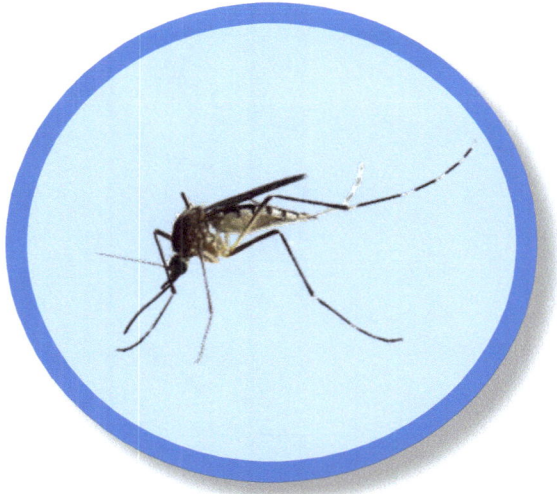

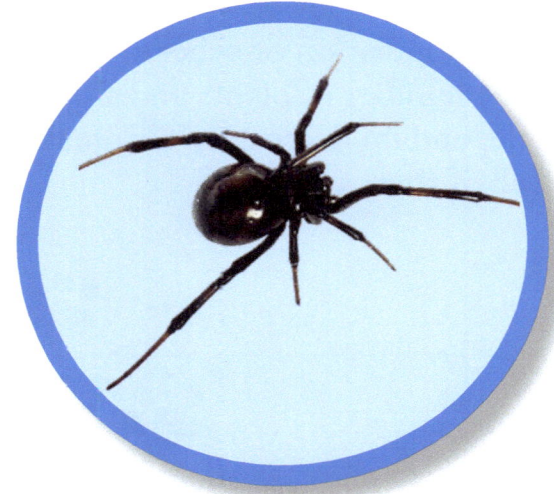

What do all these have in common? Each of them causes more harm to humans than wolves.

Most of all, wolves are important to our world. They help keep nature in balance. Some of the animals that wolves kill are sick or injured. Removing these animals helps keep their herds healthy.

With fewer wolves to prey upon them, the population of other animals increases. Then, the number of plants and animals those animals depend on decreases. This makes it harder for all of them to survive.

Because wolves have a critical effect on their environment, scientists consider them a **keystone species.**

Wolves will help keep this herd of elk moving so they won't eat too many of the plants. Wolves change the population, distribution, and behavior of their prey. This often changes the landscape.

Tribes of the Pacific Northwest have carved totem poles for centuries. These poles tell stories as well as celebrate histories, people, or events. Tribes often spotlight respected animals—including the wolf—on their totem poles.

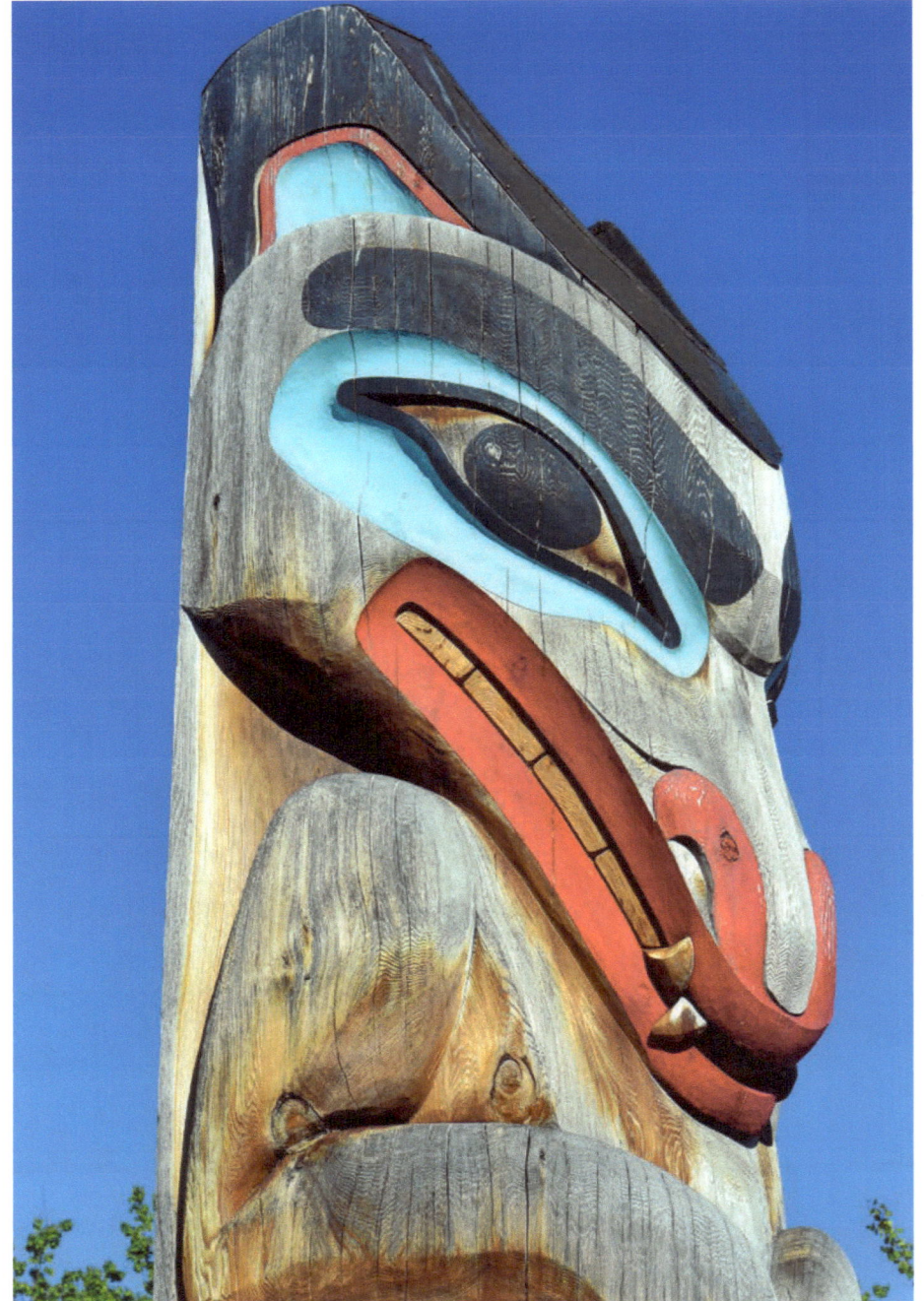

Wolves Over Time

For thousands of years wolves roamed North America. Most native tribes lived in harmony with them. Many admired the animals' strength, loyalty, and hunting skills.

In the 1600s, people from Europe came to settle North America. With them, they brought their fear and hatred of wolves. They saw wolves as dangerous and evil, something to be eliminated. So, the settlers began a war against wolves.

Why did people fear and hate wolves? The fear came from folktales and stories they heard as children. Stories like "Little Red Riding Hood" told about vicious wolves. The hatred came when hungry wolves killed livestock people raised.

In North America, rewards, called bounties, were first paid in 1630 for killing wolves. Bounties for settlers included cash, corn, tobacco, and wine. For Native Americans, the bounties were blankets and trinkets.

By the middle of the 20th century, government-sponsored wolf hunters killed nearly all the wolves in the lower 48 states.

14

So, it was the settlers against the wolves. Who do you think would win? Wolves had sharp teeth and powerful jaws, but the settlers had traps, poison, and guns. In the end, it wasn't close. The people wiped out almost all the wolves.

When people realized how few wolves were left, some wanted to protect them. These people shared the truth about wolves with others. They wrote letters to their representatives and spoke out.

The United States government acted. In 1973, Congress passed a law, the Endangered Species Act, to protect wolves and other animals at risk of becoming extinct.

Over three hundred years, hunters killed more than a million wolves in North America.

The government began working with wildlife groups that wanted to help wolves. These *friends* of the wolf rescued animals and gave them safe places to live. They raised wolves and helped put some into the wild. And, they taught people the importance of wolves.

The number of wolves grew—they grew so much that in some areas wolves were no longer protected. Hunting was made legal and the killing of wolves began again. Hunting continues today. So does the work of the *friends* of the wolf.

The number of red wolves and Mexican wolves, a type of gray wolf, are so low that they are all still protected.

Mexican gray wolf

There are two ways wolves get released in the wild. In a hard release, workers open the carrying crates and the wolves are free to leave. In a soft release, the wolves are put into a fenced pen to get used to the area first. After a few days, workers remove the fence.

Life at a Sanctuary

Workers at the California Wolf Center (CWC) are some of the many *friends* of the wolf. The CWC is a 50-acre sanctuary located in Julian, California, near San Diego.

Life at The California Wolf Center is filled with activity. The days begin early, when an animal care worker does a walk-through. The worker makes sure all the fences are secure and checks on the 28 animals. Are they all there? Do any look sick? A few of the wolves get medicine.

A sanctuary is a place where animals are cared for and protected. The California Wolf Center has provided a home to more than 150 wolves since 1977.

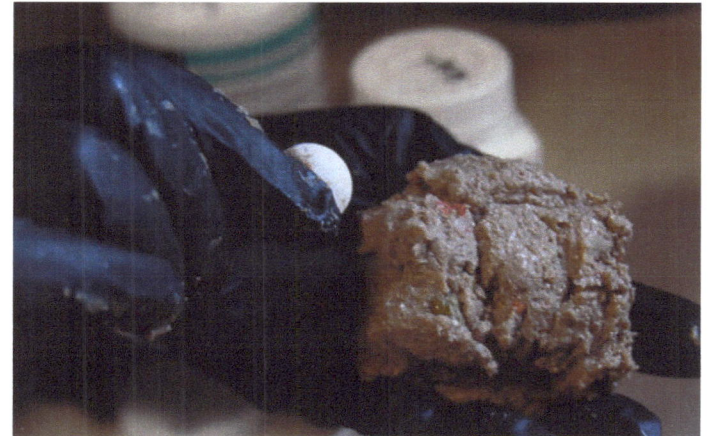

How do you get wolves to eat their medicine pills? You hide them in meatballs!

Excited visitors listen as the facility manager describes wolf biology, tells how important wolves are to nature, and explains how the CWC puts endangered wolves into the wild. He reminds visitors that wolves are wild animals and DO NOT make good pets. Then, he leads visitors out to the enclosures to observe the wolves.

There are two groups of wolves here: the non-release wolves and the release wolves. The non-release wolves will never live outside the sanctuary. The staff uses them to show and teach visitors. The release wolves—all Mexican gray wolves—might be put into the wild, so it is important they have little contact with humans. Visitors do not see them.

Being around humans makes wolves less afraid of them. Fear of humans helps wolves survive in the wild.

Not all types of wolves are the same. The presenter shows visitors skulls from a Mexican gray wolf (left) and a Rocky Mountain gray wolf (right).

A wheelbarrow
is a useful tool
at feeding time.

It's feeding time at The California Wolf Center! The wolves get food three days a week, like they would probably get in the wild. Non-release wolves eat mainly beef, chicken, and fish. The release wolves eat fish, deer, and kibbles. Why do you think these wolves are not fed beef and chicken?

It takes about 1,500 pounds of food each week to feed the 28 wolves. That's three tons of food a month (6,000 pounds) and 36 tons (72,000 pounds) every year. That's the equivalent of about 288,000 burgers!

On some days, wolves get special treats to stimulate their bodies and minds. These treats range from herbs, hard-boiled eggs, watermelons, and ice pops to frozen rats and deer antlers.

Have you ever had a clam ice pop? Wolves love them! Workers mix pieces of clams with water and freeze them in cardboard cups. Then they pop the frozen mixture out of the cups and toss them to the wolves.

More visitors arrive during the day. While they learn, workers are busy at the sanctuary. Some maintain the buildings and grounds. Others prepare food, clean wolf enclosures, make sure the animals have water, or share wolf information with the world.

Not all the work these *friends* of the wolf do is on-site. Sanctuary staff visit ranches that have wolves living near them. To help the ranchers keep their animals safe, the staff share tips and techniques: use fencing, fladry (small, colorful flags), loud sounds, lights, guard dogs, and range riders.

Each year the director of the CWC attends a special meeting. Representatives from the U.S. and Mexican governments as well as wolf organizations attend to make decisions about the endangered wolves. Which ones will be bred? Which ones will be put into the wild? Decisions are based on the family background of the wolves as well as their health and behavior.

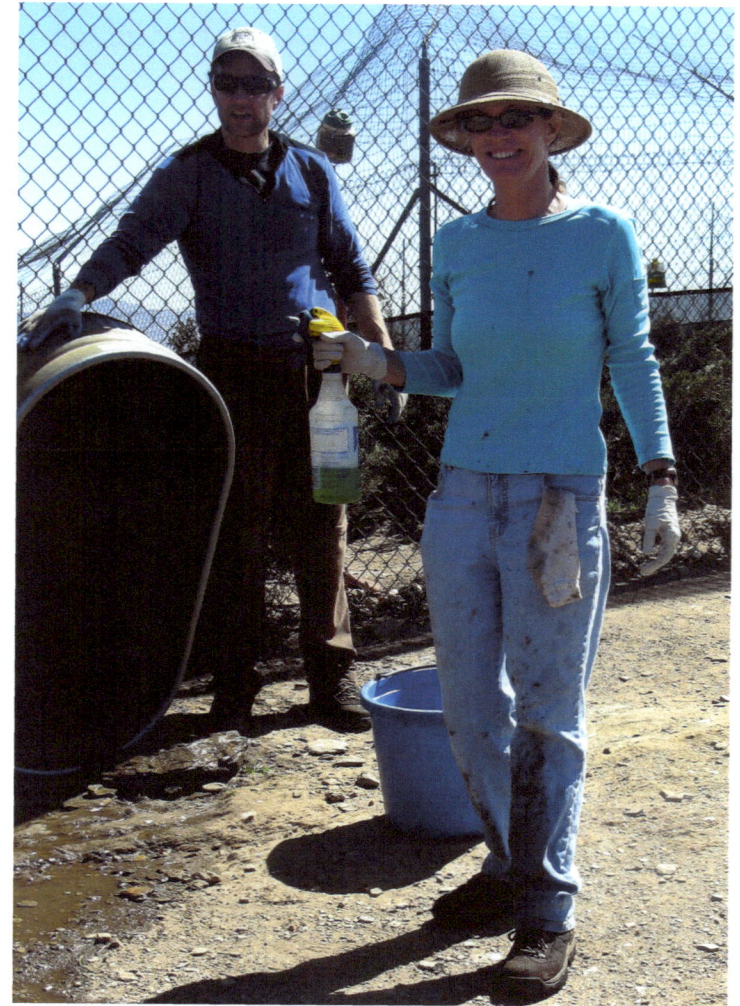

Cleaning the troughs helps keep the wolves' water supply healthy.

The most effective way to protect livestock is to use range riders (and dogs) to oversee herds and keep the animals safe.

To keep a wolf in place, workers gently place Y-poles against its shoulder and hip. Putting a towel over the wolf's head helps keep it calm.

If wolves are chosen for breeding, their pups are born in the spring. Six weeks later, a worker crawls into the den and gently pulls them out. A veterinarian gives the pups their first exams. After two more six-week exams, they are checked annually with the other wolves at the sanctuary.

Checking an older wolf takes teamwork. Workers enter the pen, form a line, and walk toward the wolf. The wolf either backs into a corner or enters a small wooden pen, the "wolf house." Workers use special tools to help keep the wolf in place so the vet can care for it.

Days end at the California Wolf Center like they begin, with a walk-through. Animals are counted, fences checked. Soon enough, darkness comes. And with it, the howls of the wolves.

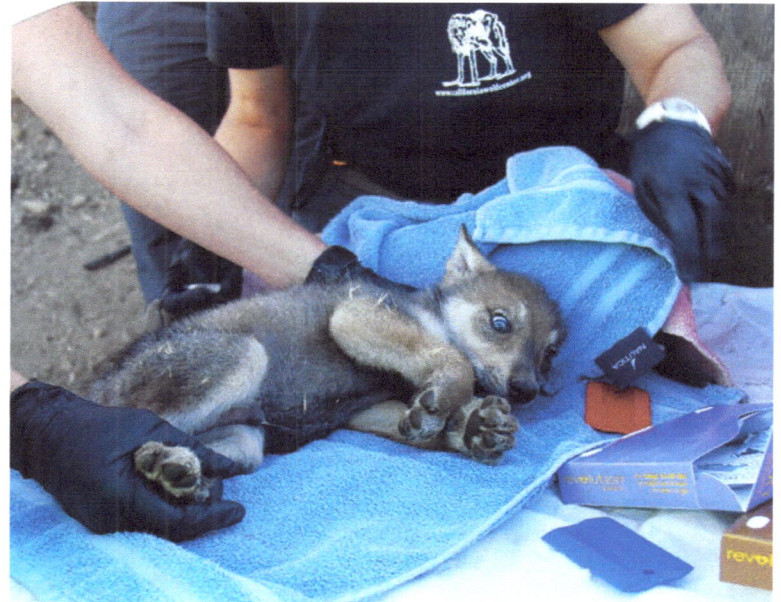

A veterinarian examines the wolf pups, takes blood samples, and gives shots.

There are about 250 Mexican wolves in sanctuaries and about 115 in the wild. Why aren't more of these wolves put into the wild? Because states in the U.S. and Mexico, which must give permission for wolves to be released there, are reluctant.

Did You Know...

A wolf pack's territory varies, up to 1,000 square miles (1,609 sq. km), the size of Rhode Island. Territory size depends on the climate, number of wolves in the pack, and the available prey.

There are two main kinds of wolves: gray (Canis lupus) and red (Canis rufus). Some scientists believe there is another type—Abyssinian (Canis simensis)—that lives in Ethiopia.

Wolf fur is made up of two layers: the soft undercoat that provides insulation and the stiff outer guard hairs that shed water.

Wolves range in color from mixtures of grays, blacks, tans, browns, and reds to all-black or all-white.

An average-size North American male gray wolf weighs from 70 to 130 pounds (32 to 59 kg), stands 26 to 36 inches (66 to 91 cm) at the shoulders, and stretches five to six feet (2 to 1.8 m) from the nose to the tip of its tail. Females are about 20 percent smaller.

Wolves are born at only one time of the year: spring. Each litter has four to six pups, and each pup weighs about a pound (.5 kg).

Subspecies (types) of gray wolves: Arctic wolf (Canis lupus arctos), eastern timber wolf (Canis lupus lycaon), Great Plains wolf (Canis lupus nubilus), Mexican wolf (Canis lupus baileyi), and Rocky Mountain wolf (Canis lupus occidentalis)

The average lifespan of a wolf is seven years in the wild and twelve years in captivity.

Become A Friend of the Wolf

You can be a _friend_ of the wolf, too. Here's how:

✓ Learn as much as you can about wolves. Read books and explore the websites listed at the back of this book. The more you learn, the better _friend_ you can be.

✓ As you learn, spread the word about wolves. Tell your family and friends how important wolves are. Share with your teacher and the kids in your class. Let them know about wolves' important role in nature. Tell them there is little to fear about wolves.

✓ Use your writing skills to share what you know. Write to your relatives. Send letters or e-mails to your newspapers and elected officials and make a case for protecting wolves.

✓ Most of the organizations that are _friends_ of the wolf are non-profit groups. That means that making money is not their goal. Still, they need money to operate. They have expenses, like rent and electricity and food for the animals. Much of the money they get comes from donations. You can help, too, by donating money.

Thank you for being a _friend_ of the wolf. The more _friends_ wolves have, the better chance they have of being a part of our world forever!

Resources

Books:

Face to Face with Wolves by Jim and Judy Brandenburg.
   Washington, D.C.: National Geographic, 2010.

Living With Wolves by Jim and Jamie Dutcher. Washington, D.C.:
   National Geographic, 2016.

Lobos by Brenda Peterson. Seattle, WA: Sasquatch Books, 2018.

Mission: Wolf Rescue by Kitson Jazynka. Washington, D.C.: National
   Geographic, 2014.

What If There Were No Gray Wolves? by Suzanne Slade. Mankato,
   MN: Picture Window Books, 2010.

Wolves by Laura Marsh. Washington, D.C.: National Geographic, 2012.

Wolves by Seymour Simon. New York: HarperCollins, 2009

Wolves by Teresa Wimmer. Mankato, MN: Creative Education, 2010.

Organizations

*California Wolf Center, Julian, CA
https://www.californiawolfcenter.org/

*Endangered Wolf Center, St. Louis, MO
http://www.endangeredwolfcenter.org/

*Lakota Wolf Preserve, Columbia, NJ
http://www.lakotawolf.com/

Living with Wolves
https://www.livingwithwolves.org/

*Mission: Wolf, Westcliffe, CO
http://www.missionwolf.org/

United States Fish & Wildlife Service
**   Gray Wolves**
https://www.fws.gov/home/wolf recovery/

**   Mexican Gray Wolves**
https://www.fws.gov/southwest/es/mexican wolf/

**   Red Wolves**
https://www.fws.gov/southeast/wildlife/mammals/red-wolf/

*White Wolf Sanctuary, Tidewater, OR
http://www.whitewolfsanctuary.com/

*Wolf Conservation Center, South Salem, NY
http://nywolf.org/

Wolf Education and Research Center,
University Place, WA
www.wolfcenter.org

*Wolf Haven International, Tenino, WA
http://wolfhaven.org/

*Wolf Park, Battle Ground, IN
http://wolfpark.org/

*Wolfwood Refuge, Ignacio, CO
http://www.wolfwoodrefuge.org

* You can visit wolves at these places.

This book is dedicated to all the *Friends* of the Wolf. May your good work continue.

With appreciation to Karen Antikajian, Kurt Cyrus, Chris Anderson, Ryan Gfroerer, Jeremy Heft, Sheri LaBat, Kent Laudon, John Oakleaf, Amy Piel, Elaine Pittman, Erik Wilber, Lois White, and Peggy Young for providing information, resources, and valued feedback. Special thanks to Caleb Carroll, Michelle Engler, Erin Hunt, John Murtaugh, and Lisa Urbanek of the California Wolf Center for helping spotlight their great facility; to Lynette Slape for her patience and persistence; and to Ava Litton, Milena Young, and Tyler Young for sharing this wolf journey.

Illustration credits: Cover © istock.com/Prachanda Rawal; title page © istock.com/mirceax; p. 2 © istock.com/Satirus; p. 3 © istock.com/KeithSzafranski; p. 4 © istock.com/labrlo, p. 5 © istock.com/KenCanning; p. 6 © istock.com/jimkruger; p.7 © istock.com/Carol Gray; p. 8 © istock.com/doug4537 (mosquito), Nerthuz (cow), spxChrome (snake), Antagain (bee), GlobalP (dog), slobo (spider); p. 9 © Living with Wolves (left),© istock.com/scanrail (right); pp. 10,11 © istock.com/KenCanning; p. 12 © istock.com/andyKRAKOVSKI; p. 13 © istock.com/ZU_09; p. 14 Arizona Historical Society; p. 15 © Lynette Slape; p. 16 © California Wolf Center; p. 17 © George Andrejko, AZ Game and Fish Department; pp. 18, 19, 21, 22, 24 © California Wolf Center; p. 25 © istock.com/cgbaldauf; pp. 26, 27 © California Wolf Center, p. 28,29 © istock.com/LazyFocus; p. 31 © Robert Young; p. 32 © Lynette Slape; back cover © istock.com/DancingMan

For permission, contact Real Writing Press at areswhy@gmail.com.

**Friends
of the
Wolf**

www.ingramcontent.com/pod-product-compliance
Lightning Source LLC
Chambersburg PA
CBHW040935050426

42334CB00048B/100

9 780974 219622